ANIMALS
That Change the World!

Frogs

Ashley Lee

Explore other books at:
WWW.ENGAGEBOOKS.COM

VANCOUVER, B.C.

e→ WWW.ENGAGEBOOKS.COM

Frogs: Level 2
Animals That Change the World!
Lee, Ashley 1995 –
Text © 2020 Engage Books
Design © 2020 Engage Books

Edited by: A.R. Roumanis,
Jared Siemens, and Lauren Dick
Design by: A.R. Roumanis

Text set in Arial Regular.
Chapter headings set in Arial Black.

FIRST EDITION / FIRST PRINTING

LIBRARY AND ARCHIVES CANADA CATALOGUING IN PUBLICATION

Title: Frogs: Animals That Change the World Level 2 reader / Ashley Lee
Names: Lee, Ashley, 1995- author

Identifiers: Canadiana (print) 20200309005 | Canadiana (ebook) 20200309013
ISBN 978-1-77437-646-1 (hardcover)
ISBN 978-1-77437-757-4 (softcover)
ISBN 978-1-77437-648-5 (pdf)
ISBN 978-1-77437-649-2 (epub)
ISBN 978-1-77437-650-8 (kindle)

Subjects:
LCSH: Frogs—Juvenile literature
LCSH: Human-animal relationships—Juvenile literature

Classification: LCC QL668.E2 L44 2020 | DDC J597.8/9—DC23

Contents

What Are Frogs?

Frogs are **amphibians**. They need to live near water to survive.

KEY WORD

Amphibians: animals that have cold blood. They live both on land and in the water.

Frogs are able to jump long distances. They are very helpful to people, other animals, and Earth.

Frogs must always keep their skin wet.

A Closer Look

The largest frogs can be 13.5 inches (30 centimeters) long. The smallest frogs are only 0.4 inches (1 cm) long.

Frog tongues are sticky to help them catch insects.

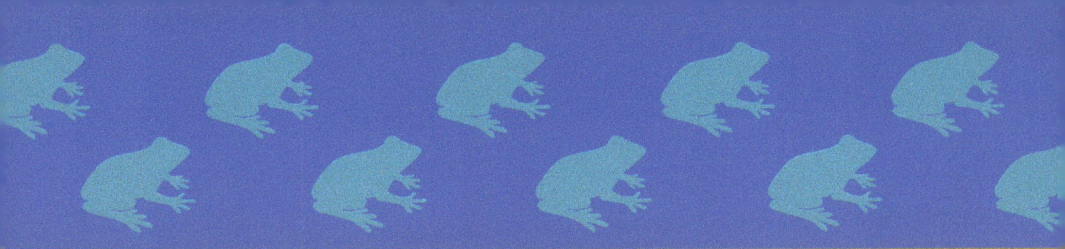

Frogs have long back legs that make them excellent jumpers.

Frogs use their webbed toes to help them swim.

Where Do Frogs Live?

Frogs live in many different **habitats**. Most frogs live in tropical areas such as rainforests. Others live in swamps, grasslands, or sand dunes.

KEY WORD

Habitats: the places a plant or animal lives. Different animals need different habitats.

Frogs can be found all over the world. Goliath frogs live in Cameroon. Purple frogs are found in the Western Ghats mountains. Iberian painted frogs are only found in Portugal and Spain.

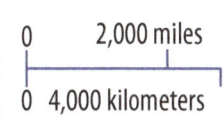

Portugal

Europe

Spain

Atlantic Ocean

Asia

Africa

Cameroon

Indian Ocean

Western Ghats

Southern Ocean

0   2,000 miles

N

0   4,000 kilometers

Legend
Land
Ocean

9

What Do Frogs Eat?

Most frogs eat insects. These may be crickets, flies, mosquitoes, or grasshoppers. They will also eat worms and slugs.

Larger frogs will eat small animals like mice or birds. Some will even eat smaller frogs.

Frog tongues move very fast. Frogs pull their food into their mouths before it has a chance to escape.

How Do Frogs Talk to Each Other?

Frogs talk to each other by croaking and chirping. Male frogs will use special calls to attract female frogs.

Some male frogs do special dances to impress female frogs. They stick their back legs out and wiggle them. Female frogs will lay eggs if they like a male frog's dance.

Frog Life Cycle

Frogs lay their eggs in the water. They can lay hundreds or thousands of eggs at one time.

Frog eggs hatch into baby frogs called tadpoles. They have tails and look like tiny fish.

Tadpoles become young frogs when they start to grow legs. Their tails become smaller. Young frogs can go on land for the first time.

Frogs become adults between 2 and 4 years old. Adult frogs have fully grown legs and no tail. They live for 5 to 8 years.

Curious Facts About Frogs

Frogs hibernate if the weather gets too cold. This means they go to sleep until the weather gets warmer.

Some frogs are poisonous. They can hurt people and other animals with just one touch.

Frogs drink water through their skin instead of their mouths.

Frogs shed their skin about every seven days. This prevents their skin from getting hard.

Frogs blink as they swallow so their eyeballs can help push down their food down.

Frogs cannot turn their heads. Their eyes let them see if anything is behind them.

17

Kinds of Frogs

There are more than 4,000 kinds of frogs all over the world. They are many different colors. Some frogs are more common than others.

Red-eyed tree frogs live in rainforests. They use their brightly colored eyes to scare other animals that might eat them.

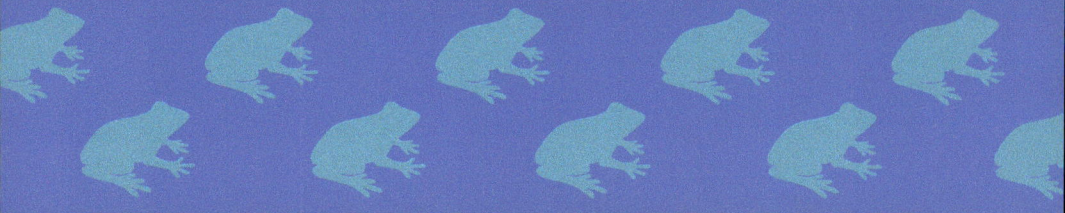

Northern leopard frogs are one of the most common frogs in North America. Their backs are covered in dark spots.

The reticulated glass frog has a see-through belly. Its beating heart can be seen through its skin.

How Frogs Help Other Animals

Frogs are an important food source for other animals. Frog eggs are food for spiders and wasps. Dragonflies, turtles, and shrimp eat tadpoles. Adult frogs provide food for birds, snakes, and lizards.

These animals would not have as much food if there were no frogs. Less food would mean less of these animals.

How Frogs Help Earth

Frogs are a sign to people that a habitat is clean and healthy. Frogs will disappear from a habitat if something is not right.

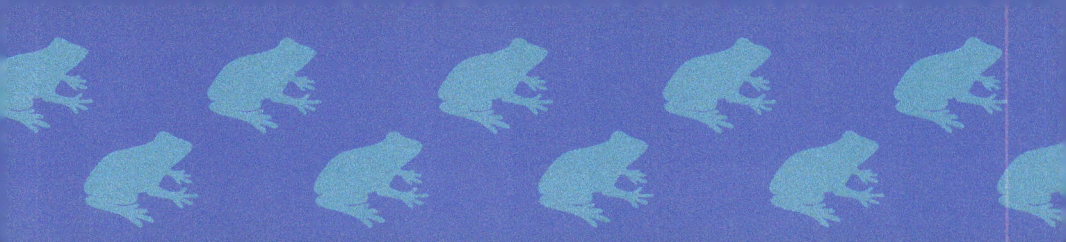

A habitat is in danger if frogs begin to disappear. Studying frogs can help scientists keep Earth clean and safe.

How Frogs Help Humans

Some insects carry diseases that they can give to humans. Frogs can eat these insects without getting sick.

Some frogs are helping doctors make new medicines. Scientists are studying frog **mucus** as a cure for human illnesses.

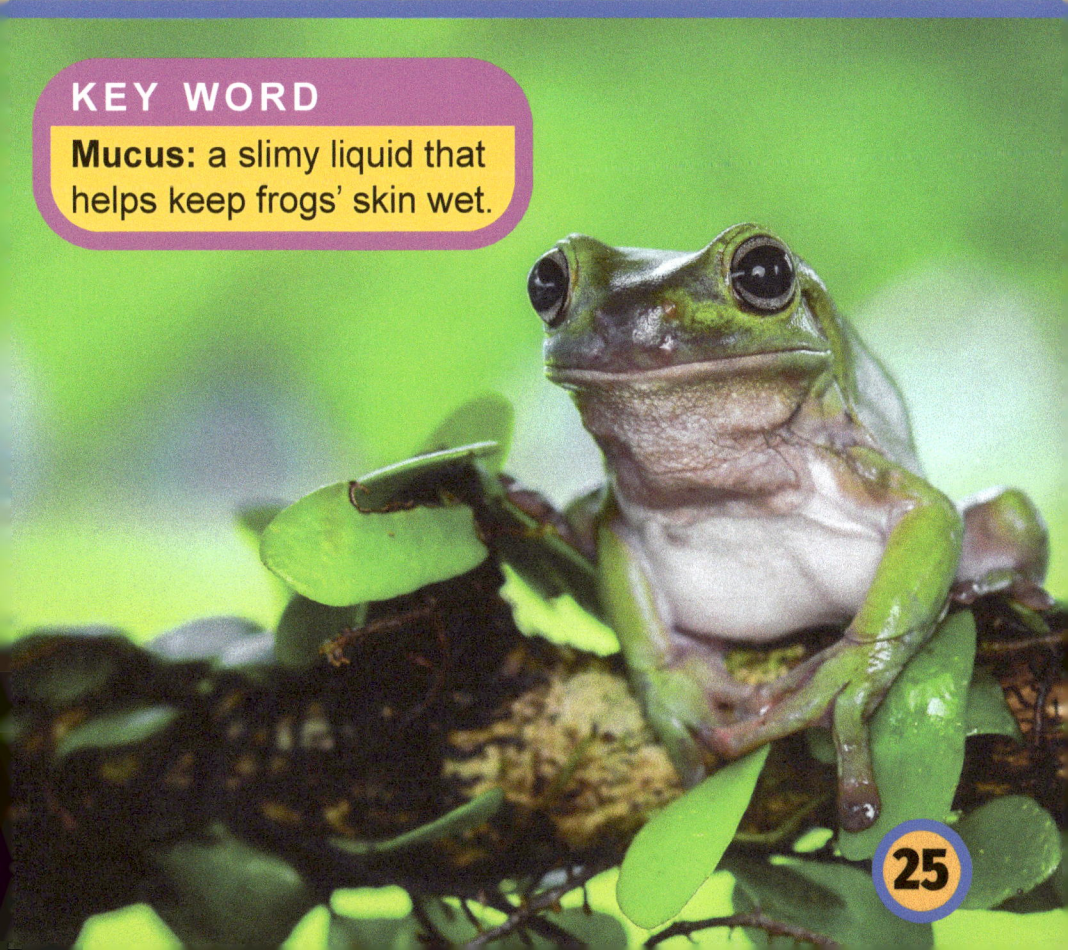

Frogs in Danger

Around 200 kinds of frogs have gone extinct since the 1970s. This means there are no more of their kind left in the world.

The Rabb's fringe-limbed tree frog went extinct in 2016. These frogs got sick from a deadly germ.

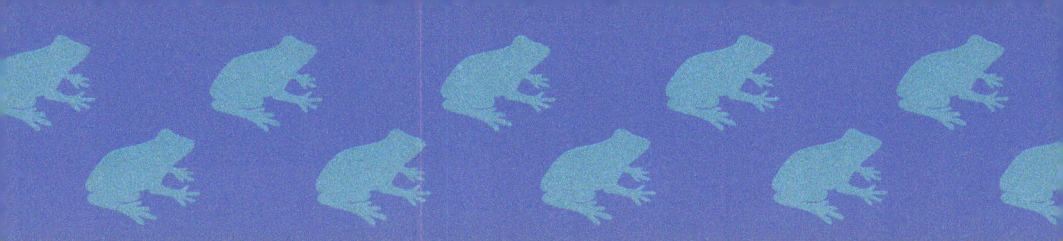

More than half of all frogs on Earth are in danger of going extinct. They are called endangered animals.

Golden mantella frogs are only found in Madagascar. Their habitat is getting smaller because of growing farms and towns.

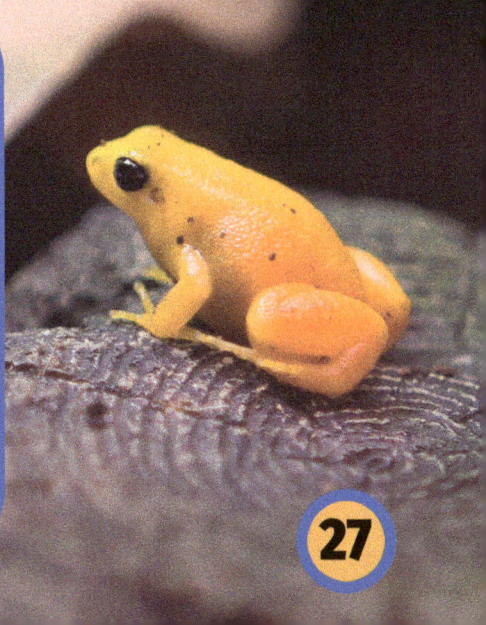

How To Help Frogs

Chemical weed and insect killers are harmful to frogs. These chemicals enter frogs' bodies through their skin. This can make them very sick.

People can help frogs by planting insect-friendly plants in the garden. Dill, marigolds, and yarrow all attract insects. This will give frogs plenty of food and places to hide.

Quiz

Test your knowledge of frogs by answering the following questions. The questions are based on what you have read in this book. The answers are listed on the bottom of the next page.

1 Where do frogs live?

2 What do frogs eat?

3 What are baby frogs called?

4 How do frogs drink water?

5 How often do frogs shed their skin?

6 How many kinds of frogs have gone extinct since the 1970s?

Explore other books in the Animals That Change the World series.

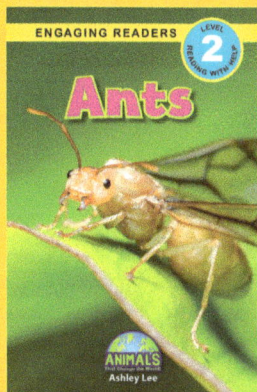

ENGAGING READERS — LEVEL 2 — READING WITH HELP
Ants
ANIMALS That Change the World
Ashley Lee

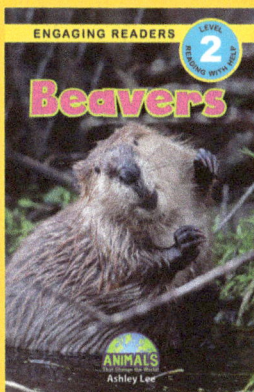

ENGAGING READERS — LEVEL 2 — READING WITH HELP
Beavers
ANIMALS That Change the World
Ashley Lee

ENGAGING READERS — LEVEL 2 — READING WITH HELP
Butterflies
ANIMALS That Change the World
Ashley Lee

ENGAGING READERS — LEVEL 2 — READING WITH HELP
Dogs
ANIMALS That Change the World
Ashley Lee

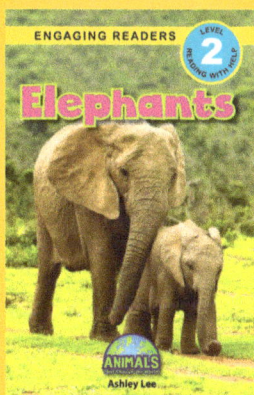

ENGAGING READERS — LEVEL 2 — READING WITH HELP
Elephants
ANIMALS That Change the World
Ashley Lee

ENGAGING READERS — LEVEL 2 — READING WITH HELP
Frogs
ANIMALS That Change the World
Ashley Lee

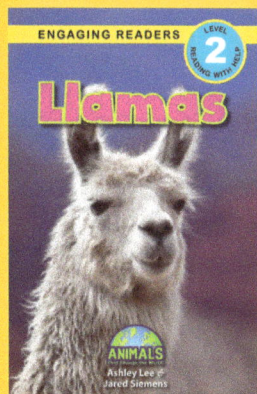

ENGAGING READERS — LEVEL 2 — READING WITH HELP
Llamas
ANIMALS That Change the World
Ashley Lee &
Jared Siemens

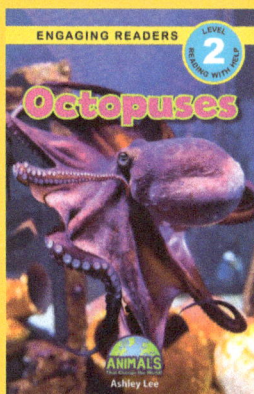

ENGAGING READERS — LEVEL 2 — READING WITH HELP
Octopuses
ANIMALS That Change the World
Ashley Lee

ENGAGING READERS — LEVEL 2 — READING WITH HELP
Primates
ANIMALS That Change the World
Ashley Lee

Visit www.engagebooks.com to explore more Engaging Readers.

Answers: 1. Rainforests, swamps, grasslands, or sand dunes 2. Insects and small animals 3. Tadpoles 4. Through their skin 5. About every seven days 6. Around 200

www.ingramcontent.com/pod-product-compliance
Lightning Source LLC
Chambersburg PA
CBHW051236020426
42331CB00016B/3400